# RACING FAMILIES

# RACING FAMILIES

## A Tribute to Racing's Fastest Dynasties

TOM GILLISPIE

FOREWORD BY
BOBBY ALLISON

Beckett Publications
Dallas, Texas

Published by:
Beckett Publications
15850 Dallas Parkway
Dallas, Texas 75248

ISBN: 1-887432-87-6

Beckett® is a registered trademark of Beckett Publications.

First Edition: March 2000
Beckett Corporate Sales and Information (972) 991-6657

Jacket design: Rick Carnes
Book design: Hespenheide Design

Photo credits: p.128

# CONTENTS

# All in the Family

BY  BOBBY  ALLISON

Really, racing was the perfect deal. Racing was the one activity where you could include the whole family, at least for part of it.

My wife would go along and be involved. Some of the wives were scorers in the old days. The youngsters could be around the race cars. There was an age limit in the garage area, and, when Davey was really young, we'd have to sneak him into the garage area once in a while. But pretty early on, NASCAR allowed special permission for ones they were confident would stay where they needed to stay and do the right things.

The whole family, the sons and the daughters, could be interested in what was going on. The equipment was interesting. The fact that other families got involved help the girls enjoy it. It was really the perfect family activity.

Davey and Clifford were quite different from each other. Davey was so committed and so focused on racing that he was almost aggravating. With Clifford, one week racing was important to him, the next week it might be some ball sport, roller skating or going out with his buddies some- where. Clifford was into everything, where Davey was focused on racing, but it gave me pleasure to see Davey that interested in racing that early and really work toward trying to develop a career.

I felt like I always spent a lot of time with them, but I couldn't spend one hundred percent of the time with them. After they got involved in

their careers, I was able to spend more time with Davey, but then he went and did his thing, and I went and did my thing.

As racing developed into a more professional and more attractive activity to the world, it certainly added to the quality of our family life and our life away from the racetrack. I don't know of anything that I would have changed. I enjoyed my career and got to do some unusual things. We saw a lot of the country as we did the race circuit.

The kids got together a lot more than the parents did. They had a lot of time that was similar,

"The whole family, the sons and the daughters, could be interested in what was going on. It was really the perfect family activity." — Bobby Allison

so they spent a lot of time together. They had a lot of friendships; Dave and Kyle Petty were especially good friends.

Several of the youngsters fell into the group where they horsed around together, played around together. They watched the race together, and they cheered for different people in the race, but that was secondary. Davey and Kyle had no part of the rivalry between Bobby Allison and Richard Petty.

I recently watched an old video of me and Davey. That talked about the rivalry a little bit, and I got a kick out of that. I thought about some early days when the kids were out there. We were working and they were over there having some recreation, some time together. It developed into some friendships that are, or would be, strong today.

The thing is that racing and family go together. Anybody in that garage area will help just about

Bobby used to sneak Davey into the garage area when he was younger, but when Davey won the 1992 Daytona 500, his wife and kids were more than welcome in victory lane.

anybody else in that garage area. If somebody needs help, it's almost always available from everybody else. It's like a big family within a big family.

*Bobby Allison knows all about racing and how it affects a family, both positively and negatively. The long-time resident of Hueytown, Alabama, led the so-called "Alabama Gang," which featured Bobby's brother Donnie, Red Farmer and Neil Bonnett as main members. Bobby's older son, Davey, won nineteen Winston Cup races, including the 1992 Daytona 500, and died in 1993 while landing a helicopter at Talladega [Alabama] Superspeedway. Bobby's other son, Clifford, died in a crash at Michigan Speedway. Bobby, the winner of eighty-three Winston Cup races and the 1983 championship, is a member of several racing halls of fame.*

*Tom Gillispie interviewed Allison for this foreword.*

# BLOODLINES

## THE PETTYS

**Lee:** won Winston Cup championships in 1954, 1958 and 1959 and recorded fifty-four victories.

**Richard:** seven-time Winston Cup champion and NASCAR's winningest driver with two hundred victories.

**Kyle:** eight-time winner on the Winston Cup circuit.

**Adam:** representing the fourth generation of Pettys on the Winston Cup tour with five scheduled races in 2000.

## THE JARRETTS

**Ned:** Winston Cup winner in 1961 and 1965 before retiring at age thirty-four.

**Dale:** the 1999 Winston Cup champion, Dale won eighteen races from 1996 to 1999.

**Glenn:** short-lived racing career gave way to broad-casting career. Glenn serves as a commentator and reporter for TNN and TBS.

**Jason:** Dale's son, entered the 2000 season on the Busch Grand National circuit.

## THE EARNHARDTS

**Ralph:** Hall of Famer won thirty-two races and the national Modified championship in 1956.

**Dale:** winner of seven Winston Cup titles and more than $35 million in career earnings.

**Dale Jr.:** two-time Busch Grand National champion gunning for rookie of the year honors on the Winston Cup circuit in 2000.

**Kerry:** BGN and ARCA driver.

## THE ALLISONS

**Bobby:** eighty-four race winner and 1983 Winston Cup champion led at least one lap for thirty-nine consecutive races.

**Donnie:** Bobby's brother won ten Winston Cup races and still serves as a racing consultant.

**Davey:** won nineteen races and contended for the Winston Cup title before dying in a 1993 helicopter accident.

**Clifford:** Davey's brother, died from injuries sustained in a crash while practicing at Michigan Speedway in 1991.

## THE LABONTES

**Bob:** father and mentor who started sons Terry and Bobby in quarter-midget racing at a young age.

**Terry:** two-time Winston Cup champion (1984 and 1996) who entered the 2000 season with a record 637 consecutive starts.

**Bobby:** won a career-high five races in 1999 en route to second place in the Winston Cup standings.

## THE ANDRETTIS

**Mario:** tied with A.J. Foyt for "Driver of the 20th Century" honors by the Associated Press in 1999, thanks to a career that included four Indy-car championships.

**Michael:** the winningest active driver on the CART circuit with thirty-eight career victories.

**John:** son of Mario's brother, Aldo, John is the only driver to win a Winston Cup race, Indy-car event and a twenty-four-hour race at Daytona.

**Jeff:** a former Indy rookie of the year.

EARNHARDT WINS THE 1999 DIE HARD 500 AT TALLADEGA

DALE JR. RACES THE #8 BUDWEISER CAR

**Fonty:** won nineteen Winston Cup races and finished second twenty times.

**Carl:** raced boats before switching to the real estate business.

**Ethel:** stock car driver and part owner of car driven by Tim.

## THE FRANCES

**Bill Sr.:** racer and promoter who was the impetus behind the formation of the National Association for Stock Car Auto Racing.

**Bill Jr.:** chairman of the board and chief executive officer of the powerful International Speedway Corporation.

**Jim:** President of the ISC.

**Lesa Kennedy:** Executive Vice President of the ISC.

**Brian:** Senior Vice President of Marketing and Communications of NASCAR.

## THE UNSERS

**Bobby:** won thirty-five Indy-car races, as well as the Indianapolis 500 three times.

**Al Sr.:** two-time Indy-car champion and four-time Indianapolis 500 winner.

**Al Jr.:** an Indy-car champion in 1990 and 1994 who has posted thirty Indy-car wins.

**Louis:** won the Pikes Peak Hill Climb nine times.

**Joe:** killed early during his career test driving a FWD Coleman Special.

**Jerry:** died at twenty-seven following crash at Indy.

**Johnny:** competed in fourteen IRL races in 1999, finishing in the top ten twice.

**Robby:** won the Pikes Peak climb in 1990.

## THE BAKERS

**Buck:** former bus driver who won Winston Cup championships in 1956 and 1957.

**Buddy:** won forty poles and nineteen Winston Cup races and is a member of the International Motorsports Hall of Fame.

## THE BODINES

**Geoffrey:** Daytona 500 winner in 1986 and named one of NASCAR's "50 Greatest Drivers" in 1998.

**Brett:** longtime Winston Cup driver and owner who won a Modified championship in 1984.

**Todd:** entered the 2000 season with ten Busch Grand National victories.

**Barry:** Geoffrey's son has driven on the Craftsman Truck circuit and filled in for dad on the BGN series.

## THE BURTONS

**Ward:** consistent driver who placed ninth in the 1999 Winston Cup standings.

**Jeff:** finished fifth in the Winston Cup standings in 1999 with six victories.

## THE WALLACES

**Russ:** recreational racing spurred sons Rusty, Mike and Kenny to make driving their careers.

**Rusty:** won forty-nine races through 1999, including the 1989 Winston Cup championship.

**Mike:** former Winston Cup driver who placed sixth in the 1999 Craftsman Truck series standings.

**Kenny:** eight-time BGN winner who claimed three top-five finishes on the Winston Cup circuit in 1999.

## THE FLOCKS

**Bob:** won four Winston Cup races in thirty-six career starts.

**Tim:** the most successful Flock brother who won Winston Cup championships in 1952 and 1955.

## THE WALTRIPS

**Darrell:** three-time Winston Cup points champ who entered his 2000 farewell tour with eighty-four career wins.

**Michael:** has earned more than $9 million on the Winston Cup circuit without a points victory.

# FIRST FAMILIES

# The Pettys

> "The only gene that's the same in all of us is the love of the sport, the love of driving race cars and being around racing people."
>
> — Kyle Petty

**I**t's never been easy being the Pettys. There's the fan adulation, the injuries — the expectations.

Lee, Richard and Kyle Petty are well aware of the ups and downs of the life they've chosen. Certainly, they've won many races, but they also have endured long dry spells when victory eluded all their efforts.

After the 1999 season, their most recent drought appears to be ending.

Petty Enterprises is back on the upswing, with Kyle racing Winston and Adam Petty, Kyle's son, racing Busch Grand National for Richard. Adam made his Winston Cup debut in 2000, becoming the fourth generation of the family to race in the big time.

With team driver John Andretti also winning in Winston Cup and Jimmy Hensley taking the checkered flag in the family's Craftsman Truck Series Dodge, the Pettys are back in victory lane and in the limelight — where they seemingly were always meant to be.

It's hard to imagine it, but there was a time when little was expected of the Pettys. Lee, for instance, drove the family car — a 1948 four-door Buick Roadmaster — from Level Cross, North Carolina, to nearby Charlotte. With half the fam-

ily riding along, Lee found a Texaco station, put the car up on a rack, changed the oil, greased the car, checked the tire pressure and headed for the board-paved Charlotte Speedway for NASCAR's first sanctioned race.

About halfway through the race, Lee broke a swaybar, busted a tire and turned the Buick over. Lee's wife wasn't thrilled when the family was forced to hitchhike home. They would have to come back and get the damaged car later in the week.

Lee still had to make his name, though, and that came in the first Daytona 500 in 1959. A photo-finish with Johnny Beauchamp took NASCAR a couple of days to determine a winner, but third-place finisher Joe Weatherly was running almost three-wide with Petty and Beauchamp.

Weatherly, in a lapped car, could look over and see that Petty had won.

And a legend had begun. Lee Petty would have a monster career: Winston Cup titles in 1954, 1958 and 1959; the seventh-most victories ever, fifty-four; and $209,780 in winnings over sixteen years.

The best was yet to come. But, oddly, when Richard Petty started out, he wasn't even Richard Petty.

"When Richard Petty came along, he was Lee's son, and that's what they referred to him as for years," says son Kyle, who turned thirty-nine in 1999. "When he went north, he was called Dick Petty; he wasn't even Richard Petty, he was Dick Petty. He went through that stage, and then he found out who he was; he was Richard Petty."

Richard won his first Winston Cup season championship in 1964, a year in which he won nine of sixty-one races. When Richard won his fifty-fourth Winston Cup race, he and Lee were tied for the most wins ever.

Then Richard won and won and won some more. His twenty-seven victories (including ten straight) in 1967, earned him "The King" moniker and forever put him on another plane from other stock-car drivers. When he finally stopped winning, on Independence Day 1984, Richard had taken the checkered flag two hundred times.

He'd won seven Daytona 500s and ten races overall at Daytona, both records. His seven championships ties him with Dale Earnhardt. But while Earnhardt also possesses

Under Richard's watch, Petty Enterprises made strides in 1999. In Winston Cup John Andretti claimed one victory and ten top-ten finishes while Kyle Petty finished in the top ten nine times. Jimmy Hensley also won and cracked the top ten in the Craftsman Truck standings, and Adam Petty prepared for the part-time move to Winston Cup by earning three top-fives on the Busch circuit.

legendary status, Petty is special. Even Kyle calls him The King or King Richard. So does Earnhardt.

He's been to nearly every Winston Cup race ever run, and he ran in more than 1,100 of them. Naturally, that's a record.

"I am history," he said during NASCAR's 50th anniversary celebration in 1998. "My family, the Pettys, we are NASCAR history. I'm NASCAR history whether I want to be or not. They talk about all the changes in the sport over the years and this and that, but man, I was there."

Richard Petty became the unofficial spokesman for NASCAR, and fans came in droves to get his painstakingly perfect, calligraphy-like autograph.

Whereas Lee Petty was one of the pioneers of the sport, Richard Petty was the Babe Ruth or Red Grange of auto racing, the man who carried it to another level.

The King was the first driver to have a year-long going-away party, his 1992 Fan Appreciation Tour, and he remains one of the biggest draws for autograph and merchandise collectors.

Over the years, the Petty Look — the mustache, the cowboy hat, the cowboy boots, the sunglasses — has evolved. It wouldn't be complete, of

It's hard to fathom now, but there was a time when Richard was the "other" Petty in racing. Father Lee (left) blazed a championship trail by winning Winston Cup titles in 1954, 1958 and 1959.

Richard won nine races en route to his first championship in 1964, then earned the right to be called "King" with twenty-seven wins — including ten consecutive triumphs — in 1967.

course, without the famous Petty Grin. All of the Petty men have it.

Legend has it that Kyle was in a restaurant with a group that included Richard. The King had put his hat down to eat, so Kyle put it on. Then he put on the shades . . . and he grinned.

Everyone was stunned at the similarity.

The thing is, though, it's easier for Kyle to look like Richard than vice versa. Richard isn't into any look that involves piercing a body part.

In early 1999, Kyle and Richard joked about their differences and similarities. Richard was sporting shaggy, almost Kyle-like hair, and a chin beard that matched his son's. "I'm a Kyle Petty clone," he said, "but I don't have an earring." As media members laughed, Kyle chimed in, "But you don't have a ponytail [either]," to which Richard answered, "I can have a pony tail, but I won't have an earring."

When Kyle came up in 1979, he won his first race, an ARCA event at the place that had made Lee and Richard famous: Daytona International Speedway. But Kyle quickly ran Winston Cup full-time because Richard had Winston Cup cars and Winston Cup people. They *had* to run Winston Cup.

Richard won seven Daytona 500s, including the 1979 race. His final Daytona 500 farewell came in 1992.

Richard celebrated Independence Day in 1984 by winning the Firecracker 400, his two hundredth and last Winston Cup victory. Ronald Reagan, the first President to attend a NASCAR race, was on hand.

Later, Kyle raced for the Wood Brothers, car owner Felix Sabates and himself, among others, and now he's back with Petty Enterprises.

And, though Kyle hasn't put up the big victory numbers, he's had a big-time career. He'd won eight races prior to 2000, including one at a road course, and he's shown ability at all the types of tracks: carburetor restrictor-plate, superspeedway, short track and road course. His career earnings are approaching the $10 million mark, and, while he continues to race, he's already begun to take over the everyday reins for Petty Enterprises.

Kyle, like his father and grandfather, is thinking to the future.

Adam Petty, Kyle's teen-age son, is doing his apprenticeship in Grand National while driving a Petty Enterprises car, and he plans to run five Winston Cup races in 2000 to become the first fourth-generation driver in the series.

Adam may have neither an earring or a ponytail. Or a chin beard. He might not even match his dad's eight Winston Cup victories, much less Lee's fifty-four or Richard's two hundred. But Adam has the Petty Grin, the trademark thin frame and a gift for gab. He has the Petty height. In fact, he'd probably be taller than the six-foot-three Richard if he'd wear the old man's cowboy boots.

Adam was successful in his first Grand National race at Daytona, finishing sixth, but everyone agrees that Adam won't face the media blitz that Kyle barely survived twenty-one years ago. "I was always Richard Petty's son," Kyle has said, "but I was never Richard Petty. And I went through a lot of down times and things and suddenly people said, 'That's Kyle. He's just different than Richard.'"

Indeed he is. Kyle tried a singing career years ago. He's one of the better thinkers and talkers in Winston Cup — plus, he's brash and often irreverent — so, naturally, media members often go to him when they want a spin on something.

As Winston Cup's rebel with a cause, Kyle has held an annual cross-country motorcycle trip to raise money for charity. He's the only driver who has worn long hair and earrings for years. But he figures that's all right. He's just Kyle.

"Well, Richard was different from Lee, and Adam's different from all three of us," Kyle says. "And I think we all look at life different. We're not clones of each other in any way. The only gene that's the same in all of us is the love of the sport, the love of driving race cars and being around racing people.

The King turned his full attention to running a successful racing team in 1993.

PETTY ENTERPRISES

Adam — at least so far — hasn't faced the kind of pressure his father, Kyle, weathered while racing with the Petty name. "I was always Richard Petty's son," Kyle says, "but I was never Richard Petty."

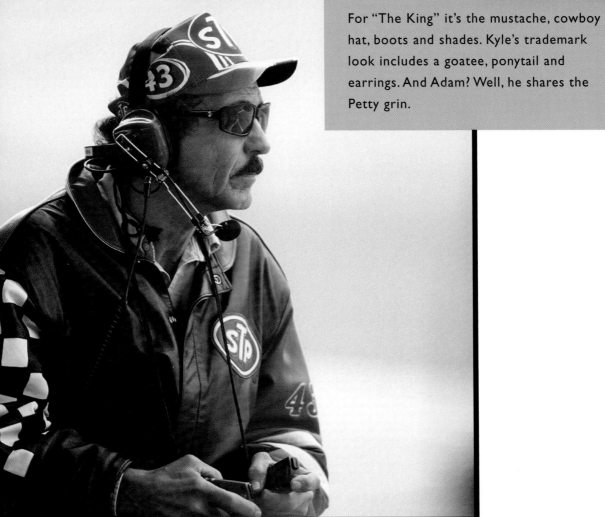

For "The King" it's the mustache, cowboy hat, boots and shades. Kyle's trademark look includes a goatee, ponytail and earrings. And Adam? Well, he shares the Petty grin.

Kyle hasn't enjoyed the same success as his legendary father — who has? — but the third racing Petty still has enjoyed a respectable career that has included eight victories and more than $11 million in earnings.

"If you ask us one question, you'll get four different answers."

Richard doesn't expect Adam to put up hall-of-fame numbers, but he doesn't expect him to go into the music business, either. He figures Adam will race hard, be his own man, go his own way and represent the family well.

"He's saying, 'I'm Adam Petty. I don't have to have a ponytail or grow a beard,'" Richard says, not even mentioning the cowboy hat and sunglasses. "He's going to try to take what he thinks is the best of Lee Petty, Richard Petty and Kyle Petty, folding it all into one person. Maybe you're finally going to get the total package.

"I think he can put the total package together."

The Pettys, and the family business, will continue.

Adam has taken full advantage of the knowledge Kyle and Richard can provide. "Growing up in the Petty family with my dad and my grandfather being around and giving me advice has done nothing but make it a ton easier on me," Adam said on his Web site, adampetty.com.

Richard believes Adam exhibits the best qualities of all his predecessors. "Maybe you're finally going to get the total package," he says.

# CHAPTER 2

# The Jarretts

> "He [Ned Jarrett] was my hero when I was a kid, and he's still my hero."

— Dale Jarrett

> "I am proud of the person he [Dale Jarrett] is off the track. What he does on the track is a bonus."

— Ned Jarrett

**T**he Jarretts are a racing family, plain and simple.

Ned Jarrett forged a hall-of-fame career that included two Winston Cup championships, and he has since been a fixture on ESPN's racing broadcasts.

Ned's son Dale is currently the hottest driver on the Winston Cup circuit after wrapping up an amazingly consistent year with the 1999 season championship.

Another son, Glenn, has worked on racing broadcasts for years. And Dale's son, Jason, who turned twenty-four on October 14, 1999, is struggling to get his career started in the Busch Grand National series.

Ned raced a couple of premier events each year from 1953 through '57. After posting two victories in sixteen races the next year, Jarrett hit the circuit full-bore in 1959, claiming five checkered flags in forty races.

Despite winning just one race in 1961, Ned claimed a Winston Cup championship. He amassed another forty-two wins during the next

1999
NASCAR WINSTON CUP CHAMPION
DALE JARRETT

four years, capping off the run with the 1965 Winston Cup points title.

But ask Ned about the highlight of his career, and he might mention something that happened while he was in the broadcast booth. When Dale Jarrett won the 1993 Daytona 500, CBS pushed Ned into rooting Dale on to victory. In the "Dale and Dale Show," Dale Jarrett edged Dale Earnhardt, and Ned exclaimed, "Come on, Dale. And you know which Dale I'm rooting for!"

Ned Jarrett was broadcasting the Daytona again in 1996 when DJ repeated his heroics against Earnhardt. The cheering was downplayed the second time, but he says he and wife Martha were happy for Dale nonetheless.

"Those were proud times for me, but they were also hard, because I'm a professional and I don't want it to sound like I'm getting personally involved," Ned says. "You walk a real difficult line in a situation like that.

"The first time, they just handed me the microphone and said, 'Bring Dale home.' The second time, I told them I didn't want to do it and they handed me the microphone again anyway. I guess it went OK."

Certainly, Ned Jarrett was excited when Dale won the '99 Winston Cup title. The Jarretts became the second father-son duo — after Lee and Richard Petty — to take the championship,

and it capped a stellar run in which Dale finished third, second, third and first in the point standings.

Dale never had the opportunity to cheer on his father on national television, but after capturing his own Cup title, he was equally thankful to his dad.

"This sport has been awful good to the Jarrett family over the years," Dale says. "To now become the second father-son team to win a Winston Cup championship is pretty special to us. Hopefully we've given a little something back to the sport. The fans have just been fantastic to us. This is just

As a race-day broadcaster, Ned Jarrett has had the opportunity to call many of his son's victories, including Dale's Daytona 500 wins in 1993 and 1996.

Little Dale (right) probably knew he wanted to race for a living following Ned's victory in the 1965 Southern 500. "The whole town was in our front yard wanting to celebrate," Dale says.

"I've been able to live a fantasy through him," Ned says of Dale. "It gives me great feelings of pride and accomplishment."

an incredible feeling, a great day for the Jarrett family. I just hope that there is more to come."

Ned says Dale the man means more to him than Dale the racer. "I am proud of the person he is off the track," Ned says. "What he does on the track is a bonus."

Besides the two Daytona 500 victories, Ned has witnessed Dale win a pair of Brickyard 400s, something he never accomplished during his own career.

"It's very special to see him win those big events that I was not able to win," says Jarrett. "To see your children do more than you did, that's more meaningful to me than when I was driving. I've been able to live a fantasy through him. It gives me great feelings of pride and accomplishment."

Dale says the feeling is mutual. "He was my hero when I was a kid, and he's still my hero," Dale says of his father. "Growing up the son of Ned Jarrett was exciting. Certainly, the sport wasn't where it is today. But it was still fun. I got to travel a lot, see and do a lot of different things.

"I think it was probably later in my dad's career — he was still a young man when he retired [at age thirty-four] — but I realized that he was doing something special and he was a special athlete."

The highlight, Dale says, was Ned's win at Darlington (South Carolina) Raceway. "I still

remember when my dad won the 1965 Southern 500 and clinched the championship at the same time," Dale says, flashing a wide grin. "I didn't realize until we got back home in Camden [South Carolina] the magnitude of what had just taken place. The whole town was in our front yard wanting to celebrate. That's when it hit me just exactly what he had done. It was great."

Occasionally, Ned will spot for Dale. After one such race, a victory, DJ talked about his father's influence. "He's been my biggest supporter," he said. "It's great to have a dad and a friend who knows enough about the sport that he can help you. He was a big help Sunday."

Ned and Dale Jarrett have been on the track together one time. A few years ago on the Winston Cup Media Tour, the Jarretts took race cars onto the one-sixth-mile track on Charlotte Motor Speedway's frontstretch. Ned had a 1966-vintage Ford that he'd raced to victory. Dale had a modern No. 88 Robert Yates Racing Ford.

They made a few laps together. Then they switched cars, with Ned driving the 88 and Dale taking out the well-kept, red-and-white Ford. Dale saw the bigger windows and noticed the steering was poor. Ned noticed the lessened visibility but reveled at the greater horsepower in the modern Ford.

"It was an eye-opener for both of us," Ned says. "It gave us additional respect that we didn't have for each other."

Interestingly, Ned says it almost didn't happen.

"Actually, I didn't think he'd become a race driver," Ned says of Dale, who had shown more interest in golf. "Once he chose auto racing as a career, he talked first about running the Winston Cup series one day. That took a while. Then once he got there, he started talking about winning a race. Then he was looking ahead to the right situation to contend for a title."

Ned says he started thinking of Dale as a title contender when Dale joined Joe Gibbs Racing in 1993. He figured it might be a few years before Dale was a serious threat, but he thought it could happen.

Dale didn't have a great start when he switched

to Robert Yates Racing. Oh, he won the 1995 Daytona 500 pole, but he won just one race while driving cars with serious horsepower. Davey Allison and Ernie Irvan had excelled in those cars, so why couldn't Dale?

The worst thing, Ned says, is that DJ was a lame-duck driver. He was hired for a year to replace the injured Irvan.

"In fact, there were some conversations that he and Robert [Yates] and [crew chief] Larry McReynolds had that opened the door for him to resign," Ned says. "Yes, there were a lot of

Once Dale joined Joe Gibbs Racing in 1993, Ned could tell his son had what it took to become a Winston Cup champion.

In 1996 Dale relinquished the No. 28 Havoline Ford to a healthy Ernie Irvan and moved into the red and blue No. 88. He's been at the top of the sport ever since.

Dale won his second Brickyard 400 in 1999 — one of four victories — en route to his first Winston Cup championship.

speculations that he didn't have what it takes and his future wasn't too bright in the sport."

Ned says the team finally realized they had not taken new rules into account, and they hadn't compensated for the fact that the six-foot-two, two hundred-pound Dale was forty to fifty pounds heavier than Irvan.

In 1996, Irvan moved back into the No. 28 Ford. Jarrett switched to the No. 88, and DJ captured his second Daytona 500 victory. He's been one of the top contenders for the title since.

And now that Dale's a bona fide champion, it's fair to compare father and son. Ned Jarrett won fifty races and is a Hall of Famer. He retired young, at thirty-four, partly because of the Fireball Roberts incident (Roberts died following a fiery crash) and similar crashes. Dale, who turned forty-three on November 26, 1999, won't win fifty races — he was at twenty-two after the 1999 season — but Ned says Dale is a better driver than he was.

"There are some similarities between the way he drives and the way I drove," Ned says. "He's

Dale waited fifteen years for his first Winston Cup points title, but it all came together in 1999. "Something my father taught me long ago was patience," Dale says.

"This sport has been awful good to the Jarrett family over the years. To now become the second father-son team to win a Winston Cup championship is pretty special to us. Hopefully we've given a little something back to the sport."
— Dale Jarrett

"That [the athletic ability] made him a better race driver than me," Ned says. "We had similarities in style. I always felt at least as good to outsmart them than to outdrive them. Dale's a thinking man's race driver, and that's important today. He's learned a lot about race cars. . . . And he realizes, like I did, that you have to finish before you can win. He doesn't take a lot of unnecessary chances."

Dale says he's glad he was able to learn from one of the best.

"Something my father taught me long ago was patience," says Dale, who began racing in 1977 in the limited sportsman division at Hickory (North Carolina) Motor Speedway, where Ned was once the track promoter. Jason, in fact, made his first Grand National series start at Hickory a few years ago. "He [Ned] showed me that it was a quality that I had within me that I had to learn to use in the right situations.

"When I first started my racing career, he didn't have the money to give me to say, 'Here, go race.' But he did help me in other ways, like helping me find sponsors. He wanted me to work on the cars and run the business.

a better athlete than me. He was born a better athlete."

In fact, Dale played football, basketball, baseball and golf in high school. Jarrett was twice named his conference's golfer of the year while at Newton-Conover High School in North Carolina. Once, Dale was coming back from surgery, Ned says, and his first day back on the links, he shot a 77.

He helped me set up [cars], but it was up to me to take it and use the money accordingly and learn the cars.

"I had to work on the cars, do the books, pay the bills, drive the truck and get to the racetrack and work on the car there. It is something that I look upon now as a benefit. And Dad knew it would be."

Dale, a father of four, once organized a NASCAR fund-raising effort that raised nearly $10,000 for the daughter of Indy Racing League driver Scott Brayton. Brayton was killed during practice for the 1996 Indy 500.

# CHAPTER 3

# The Earnhardts

"I wanted to race, that's all I ever wanted to do."

— Dale Earnhardt

In the mid-1970s, a driver was making a stirring charge through a race field, and a reporter jumped up in the pressbox and exclaimed, "Look at Earnhardt's kid!" Earnhardt back then was Ralph Earnhardt, a pretty fair country driver who won thirty-two races and the national Modified championship in 1956.

Earnhardt's kid, at that point, was Ralph Dale Earnhardt, who would win a record-tying seven Winston Cup championships, at least seventy-four Winston Cup races and more than $35 million in Winston Cup earnings through 1999. In fact, "Earnhardt's kid" is one of the winningest Busch Grand National drivers ever, one of the most successful International Race of Champions racers ever (three championships overall, three wins in 1999 alone) and the 1998 Daytona 500 champion.

After winning the Winston Cup rookie of the year title in 1979, Earnhardt became the first driver to follow up a rookie title with a Winston Cup championship, in 1980. He has gone on to win six more championships through '99, all at Richard Childress Racing (1986–87, 1990–91, 1993–94), tying him with Richard Petty for the most Winston Cup titles.

Along the way, he acquired the nicknames "The Intimidator," the "Man in Black" and "Iron-head," all reflecting his hard-charging driving style and his super-recognizable black No. 3 Chevrolets.

Half the fans love Earnhardt; the other half hate him. And when media outlets name their choices for the greatest driver ever, the short list always includes Earnhardt.

"I wanted to race, that's all I ever wanted to do," says Earnhardt, who has become a force — maybe *the* force — in collectibles. "I didn't care about work or school or anything, all I wanted to do was to work on race cars and then drive race cars. It was always my dream, and I was just fortunate enough to be able to live out that dream."

If you name the greatest moments in NASCAR history, Richard Petty's last victory, on July 4, 1984, comes to mind. So does the 1998 Daytona 500. Earnhardt had been trying in vain for two decades to win NASCAR's greatest race. He had finished second plenty of times, but he'd also run out of gas and run over a piece of bell housing.

But in '98, it all came together. Earnhardt won the race, and more than 150,000 people at Daytona

Dale grew up at the track idolizing his father. So it was no surprise that all he ever wanted to do was follow in Ralph's footsteps.

International Raceway celebrated. As Earnhardt eased down pit road, the crew members from every team lined up to high-five the champion. Earnhardt drove into infield grass for a few celebratory donuts, then returned to the receiving line for more high-fives.

Afterward, Earnhardt was asked if his career was now complete. "Hell, no, we want to win that eighth championship," Earnhardt said quickly. "That's what my life and career has been all about, winning championships. Nobody has ever won eight before, and that's what we're shooting for. We think we've got a great shot at it this year, and then we'll keep going from there."

He hasn't won No. 8 yet, but he's continued to win. He won three Winston Cup races in 1999, including both events at Talladega. He also continued his reputation as a rough driver, turning Terry Labonte on the last lap at Bristol and winning that short-track race. It was Earnhardt being Earnhardt, running to win.

Dale also got a view of his mortality. A few years ago, he passed out on the pace lap of the Southern 500 at Darlington (South Carolina)

Raceway, but tests showed that it wasn't a heart condition like the one that claimed his father in 1973. Still, it made Ironhead think.

"It was an awakening, really," he says. "A lot of people in their lives have had brushes with heart attacks, or whatever, or maybe just missing a car head on. It's something that wakes you up and makes you pay more attention, that's for sure."

Along the way, Earnhardt has become much more than just a racer. In 1999, he fielded Winston Cup Chevrolets for Steve Park, trucks for former Craftsman Truck Series champion Ron Hornaday Jr. and Grand National Chevrolets for Dale Earnhardt Jr.

In 2000, Park and Dale Jr. are driving Dale Earnhardt Inc. Winston Cup cars, while Hornaday has replaced Junior in the No. 3 Grand National cars.

Dale Jr., at twenty-five already a two-time Grand National champion, is driving Earnhardt's red-and-black Chevys as a Winston Cup rookie (using his granddad's old number, 8). Earnhardt's wife, Teresa, is listed as car owner for the Grand National team, and two of Earnhardt's other children, Kerry Dale (thirty) and Kelley King (twenty-seven), have had their own racing careers.

Dale Jr. looks like an Earnhardt kind of racer. He started out in go-karts, but he started on his road to the Cup with 113 Late Model starts at different tracks in the Carolinas. In three years competing in the NASCAR Winston Racing Series,

By finishing fifth at Riverside, the unlikely pair of Dale Earnhardt and twenty-year-old crew chief Doug Richert (left) captured the 1980 Winston Cup points title.

Earnhardt was on top of the racing world after capturing his seventh Winston Cup title in 1994 and tying Richard Petty for most Cup championships ever.

Earnhardt celebrated his 1998 Daytona
500 victory by doing donuts in the infield,
and popping champagne in victory lane.

he won three races and twelve poles. His best year
was in 1996, when he made fifty-three starts, won
eight poles and two races while finishing second
in the points at Florence (South Carolina) Motor
Speedway. He made his first career Busch Grand
National start at Myrtle Beach, where he qualified
seventh and finished a respectable thirteenth.

Then in 1998, Dale Jr.'s career took off. Dale
and Dale Jr. celebrated Junior's Grand National
crown at Homestead, and the two raced together
in the postseason exhibition race in Japan. They
were even closer in 1999, as Junior participated in
the IROC all-star series and drove Earnhardt's
Winston Cup cars for five races.

The highlight of the 1999 IROC series, other than Earnhardt's three wins and tight points victory over Mark Martin, was the Dale & Dale Show at Michigan. Dale Jr. was the leader at one point in the all-star race, but, typically, he was running hard and conservative at the same time. Suddenly, Dale Sr. dove into the mix and stole the race by inches on the last lap.

Earnhardt, not the kid, showed relief, jubilation and pride in victory lane. And Junior was thrilled to show dad that he, too, could run well.

The 1999 Busch season, though, opened not so auspiciously for Junior, but, by midseason, the youngest Earnhardt champion was back in the points lead. At the end of the season, Junior would post three straight second-place finishes and beat Jeff Green by 280 points. Junior and his team, including Dale Sr., rode around the one-mile Phoenix track in the back of a pickup truck and sprayed beer into the boisterous audience.

"It sure has been a crazy last couple of years and my life sure has changed a lot," Junior said after his second championship. "I'm thankful for all the opportunities that God has given me. I had a great time [in the Grand National Series] and we've had a lot of success."

Facing tougher competition in his first Busch Grand National circuit, Dale Jr. flourished, winning seven races en route to the points championship.

Dale and Dale Jr. raced against each other for the first time following the 1998 season in an exhibition race in Japan.

"I didn't even think about winning a championship when I came in here. I just wanted to make a good effort at it. Things started happening — I got better, we got better — and I didn't tear up a whole lot of stuff. It worked out, but all of this [winning two championships] has been a big surprise to me."

Dale Jr., in fact, was the surprise talk of NASCAR for two seasons. No one expected his 1998 championship. Heck, when he wrecked his car in the season opener at Daytona, many observers wondered if Earnhardt had erred by putting his son in the car too soon. The answer to that is, of course, no. Junior was more than up to the challenge.

Junior is inheriting the huge bloc of Dale Earnhardt fans who are still irate that Jeff Gordon usurped Earnhardt's claim as Winston Cup's top driver. And Dale Jr. already is becoming one of the biggest things in NASCAR merchandising.

No doubt the youthful, lanky, music-loving Dale Jr. will always be compared with his famous father. "Fifty percent of the time they're going to compare me to him for the good," he says, "and fifty percent of the time they're going to compare me to him for the bad."

But for every comparison that can be made between Dale and Dale Jr. on the track, another contrast can be made between their off-track demeanors.

Once Junior joined the Busch Grand National series, dad, with the backing of Dale Earnhardt Inc., was available to offer guidance every step of the way.

"A lot of the time, guys are really surprised at how different we are personality-wise," Dale Jr. says. "It's cool that it's all finally coming out. All these years, I've raced under his wing. We've never really had too much TV coverage on our races, never had too many quotes in the paper. This year I've been able to tell people things about me. It's like meeting somebody new."

A lot is expected of Dale Jr. Along with 1998 Grand National runner-up Matt Kenseth and 1999 Winston Cup rookie phenom Tony Stewart, Junior is expected to be the future of NASCAR, the man who might test — or even best — three-time Winston Cup champion Jeff Gordon.

Although Dale Jr. already has done a lot, he has a lot to live up to. Ralph Earnhardt, who died of a heart attack in 1973, was inducted into the National Motorsports Press Association Hall of Fame in 1989, the same weekend that Dale won the Southern 500 at Darlington. He was inducted into the International Motorsports Hall of Fame in

Dale Jr.'s struggles early in the 1999 season were a fluke — not his 1998 title — as Little E eventually got on track and rallied to claim his second consecutive Busch series championship.

Talladega, Alabama, in 1998 and joined Dale in being named as one of NASCAR's "50 Greatest Drivers" in NASCAR's 50th Anniversary celebration.

"This has been a very special time for me and for our family," Dale said then. "I wish he could have been here to see all of this."

In the not-so-distant future, Dale Earnhardt will leave Richard Childress Racing and concen-trate on car ownership, his farm and his other businesses. And, somewhere along the way, Dale Jr. probably will become Earnhardt, just like Grand-dad and Dad did before him.

Some fans will cheer, others will boo, and the Earnhardts will race into the future.

Ralph Earnhardt was named along with son Dale as one of NASCAR's "50 Greatest Drivers" in 1998.

Dale Jr. (right) isn't the only one of Dale's kids to find the lure of the track irresistible. Son Kerry raced on the Busch circuit for a few races in 1999. Daughter Kelley also raced Late Model Stocks on the short tracks in the Carolinas.

"It sure has been a crazy last couple of years and my life sure has changed a lot," Junior said after his second Busch Grand National championship.

Dale Jr. signed a multi-million dollar, multi-year deal with Budweiser, and expectations are high as he attempts to make the climb to the top of the Winston Cup circuit.

# CHAPTER 4

# The Allisons

The Allison family, of Hueytown, Alabama, has experienced the highest highs and the lowest lows that auto racing can provide.

During times of celebration, Bobby and Donnie Allison, along with Red Farmer, helped form the "Alabama Gang," a group of talented drivers that toured the country in search of victory. Bobby, of course, was the leader.

> "If I had kept a business chart of my racing career, it would have more peaks and valleys than the State of Arizona."
>
> — Bobby Allison

"If I had kept a business chart of my racing career, it would have more peaks and valleys than the State of Arizona," Allison has said.

Robert Arthur Allison ran a few Winston Cup races here and there in 1961 and '65, but he started his Cup career in earnest in 1966 driving a homemade Chevelle. Bobby says someone once told him he had as much chance of winning a race as slender British model Twiggy had of winning the heavyweight championship.

Three wins later, Bobby Allison had proven them they were wrong. He was a heavyweight.

Allison went on to become one of the greatest drivers in the history of NASCAR. He won eighty-four Winston Cup races, although you ask him and he'll tell you he won eighty-five. Somebody made a mistake and gave someone else a victory at Nashville.

In fact, the late T. Wayne Robertson had a story about that race in Nashville. Wayne, who later became the boss of Winston's marketing arm, was then driving NASCAR's pace car. Bobby thought he had a lap on the field. So he tried to pass Robertson under caution. He tried one side, Wayne blocked him; he tried the other, Wayne blocked him.

Finally, according to Robertson's story, Bobby put the pace car into the wall.

True or not, the story shows Allison's competitiveness. With "only" eighty-four wins, he's tied with Darrell Waltrip for third on Winston Cup's all-time list. He ranks fifth in poles won with fifty-seven, and he earned $7.1 million during an era when being a millionaire in auto racing actually meant something — not a time when Jeff Gordon might win the same amount in one year.

Astoundingly, Allison once led at least one lap for thirty-nine consecutive races, a record; and he led 29,205.2 miles, roughly the circumference of the earth. After his fortieth birthday, Allison won thirty-eight races, a total that would be fourteenth on the all-time list.

Allison was a six-time Most Popular Driver, a two-time American Driver of the Year and a

"I've been to hell and back," Bobby Allison told *The Associated Press* in 1998. "I was killed in 1988, but didn't die. Then I had to see both my sons die."

three-time National Motor-sports Press Association Driver of the Year.

In 1972, Allison started thirty-one races for car owner Junior Johnson and posted ten wins, eleven poles, and an amazing twelve second-place finishes. He didn't win the championship that year — he finished second to Richard Petty — one of five times he was runner-up in points.

Allison finally earned his only championship in 1983, when he won six races and posted five second-place finishes in thirty starts for DiGard Racing.

"Winning the championship is still my biggest thrill," Allison has said. "It's the biggest of any one thing I've ever accomplished. But it's also that I'm on par with the Pearsons, Yarboroughs, Pettys and Jarretts. It was an effort that really had started years and years before and had gone through trial after trial to get that far."

Certainly, Bobby Allison has had his trials. One of his worst came on June 19, 1988 at Pocono, where a horrific crash nearly killed him. He never raced again, and, for years, Allison's memory was impaired and selective. He once said he couldn't remember son Davey finishing second in the 1988 Daytona 500.

Over a twenty-two-year span, Allison drove for everyone from Johnson to Cotton Owens to Bud Moore to Roger Penske to Harry Ranier to the Stavola Brothers. It was a career for the ages.

But those are just facts and figures. Bobby Allison and the Allisons are about people. Bobby Allison was a fierce competitor who helped

Bobby, one of the more popular drivers in the history of NASCAR, is tied for third with Darrell Waltrip on the Winston Cup career victories list with eighty-four.

make Richard Petty "The King." Petty may have won two hundred races, including ten straight in 1967, but he needed a superb rival such as Allison or David Pearson to reach his status.

The famed "Alabama Gang," which included (from left to right) brothers Donnie and Bobby Allison and Neil Bonnett, ruled auto racing during the 1970s.

**RED FARMER**

Red Farmer, a winner of three consecutive Busch Grand National titles from 1969–71, also is an original member.

Donnie won ten Winston Cup races during a thirty-five-year racing career. He remains a part of the NASCAR scene, serving as a racing consultant.

Photographers — and CBS television cameras — caught Donnie, Bobby and Cale Yarborough trading punches after the 1979 Daytona 500, the first race television carried in its entirety.

"At one time, Richard Petty had the best car and equipment," says Allison, who once led a Hatfield and McCoy-type feud with the Pettys. "He was the goal the rest of us had to aim at; he was the target out there that set the standard."

Several years ago, Charlotte Motor Speedway was holding a "Richard Petty: This is Your Life" program during its annual media tour. Each guest would tell a story over the loudspeaker, and Richard would have to guess the anonymous person from the past. When Maurice Petty spoke, Richard appeared not to know his own brother. When another man spoke a few words, Petty jumped from his chair, and said, "That's Bobby."

The next year, the program focused on Bobby Allison, with son Davey as the master of ceremonies. Like Kyle Petty before him, Davey did a great job as MC. And like Richard Petty before him, Bobby was a popular and beloved subject.

How well regarded is Allison? Richard Petty was the first inductee to the North Carolina Auto Racing Hall of Fame. Bobby Allison, who grew up in Florida and became a legend in Alabama, was the second.

Allison was, and still is, one of the more personable people in the garage. Quick with a smile, a joke, a story, a handshake. Kind to strangers, sports writers and children.

When Allison raced, he was one of the quickest drivers to help someone in need. Need an engine? Ask Bobby. Need a trailer? Ask Bobby.

Allison once was asked why he was so helpful, and the competitive racer said with a wicked grin that he wanted to help them so he could say he helped them and beat them anyway.

Donnie didn't have quite the career of Bobby, but he was quite a driver in his own right. He finished fourth in the Indianapolis 500 one year, making him rookie of the race, and he won ten Winston Cup races.

Donnie, who still works on a Winston Cup team, was the center of the whole mess in the most acclaimed single incident in Winston Cup history. Donnie Allison appeared ready to beat a future Hall of Famer, Cale Yarborough, on the last lap of the 1979 Daytona 500, the first race that television (in this case, CBS) carried flag-to-flag.

Donnie and Cale were going down the backstretch, when Yarborough bumped Allison. The two turned slowly, crashed into the Turn 3 wall, came back across the track and stopped in the grass. As Richard Petty and Darrell Waltrip screamed past, heading for the checkered flag (Petty won), Donnie and Cale began fighting.

Bobby, who was a lap down, went around to finish the race, and then he went back around to check on Donnie. A famous photo shows a helmeted Bobby swinging above Yarborough, with Donnie apparently arbitrating the affair.

Years later, Bobby said Cale was just upset that he was going to lose the Daytona 500. Cale said it was a racing incident, and tempers flared. Bobby says he carries no animosity for Yarborough. Cale, a native of South Carolina and a winner of eighty-three Winston Cup races, claims to be an honorary member of the Allison clan and the Alabama Gang. Knowing the Allisons, you can believe him.

Davey Allison, like Donnie, didn't come close to reaching eighty-four victories, only nineteen in a career cut short because of tragedy. But he did make his father proud. Until his death in a 1993 helicopter accident at Talladega (Alabama) Superspeedway, Allison was one of the hottest drivers in Winston Cup. Davey won two races his rookie year, 1987, a Winston Cup record that held until Tony Stewart won three in 1999.

When Bobby Allison won the 1988 Daytona 500, he could look in the mirror and see Davey, the No. 2 finisher. Davey would post his own Daytona 500 victory while racing for Robert Yates Racing.

Davey, like Bobby, was a superb competitor. While Dale Earnhardt intimidated most drivers — he *is* The Intimidator, after all — Davey was one of the few drivers who would scoff at Earnhardt's bluff. Many sportswriters didn't like Davey; they thought he was short with them, giving them no time.

The 1988 Daytona 500 developed into a duel between father and son. Bobby won out, holding off Davey for the checkered flag.

But Allison also was known to give out his home number to other members of the media and was friendly and accessible to people he liked and trusted.

In 1992, Davey was a near-lock to win the Winston Cup championship. A sixth-place finish in the season finale at Atlanta would turn the trick, but Davey was involved in an early wreck and didn't finish. That gave Alan Kulwicki the title. Davey shrugged and went on.

Davey Allison claimed a narrow victory at the 1992 Daytona 500 but was edged by Alan Kulwicki for the season title. Davey mounted another charge for the Winston Cup championship in 1993 but was killed in a helicopter crash on July 13.

In 1993, Allison was mounting a tremendous challenge to Earnhardt, who was seeking his sixth Winston Cup championship. But Allison's challenge ended on July 13. Davey was flying a helicopter to Talladega, along with Red Farmer, to watch David Bonnett practice. David was the son of Neil Bonnett, another Alabama Gang member and another big-time winner.

But Davey Allison miscalculated. The helicopter crashed, and Davey later died from massive head injuries. Farmer survived, and the whole racing community mourned the loss.

Ironically, the only championship of Davey Allison's career came in the 1993 International Race of Champions all-star series. Terry Labonte drove Davey's car in the fourth and final race of the year, giving Allison the title.

Sadly, Davey wasn't the only one of Bobby and Judy Allison's sons to die in an accident. Clifford was practicing at Michigan Speedway in 1991 when he crashed and died from massive head injuries.

And Bobby Allison's torture wasn't over. Neil Bonnett had been injured in a 1990 multi-car crash at Darlington and had retired. But he couldn't stay away, running a few races here and there, just to keep his hand in. Then in February of 1994, Bonnett crashed in practice at Daytona and died.

Through it all, Bobby Allison has persevered. Bring up his boys, and Bobby will snap out his wallet to show off a picture of Davey and Clifford together.

"This picture is perfect. It shows Davey and Clifford just the way they were," Allison says, waiting for his companion to survey the photo. "You don't see it, do you?" he asks.

No, sorry.

T. Wayne Robertson testified to Bobby's competitive nature, claiming the Alabama Gang leader once crashed his pace car into the wall during a race.

Clifford Allison died after suffering massive head injuries in a crash while practicing at Michigan Speedway in 1991.

Neil Bonnett cheated death in a multi-car crash at Darlington in 1990 but didn't survive a February 1994 crash during practice at Daytona.

"Davey was being Davey," Allison says, still clutching the picture. "See, he's doing what he's supposed to do; he's smiling for the camera."

Yeah, wonderful smile.

"Look at Clifford."

Don't see it.

"Look over Davey's head. Clifford's being Clifford. He's putting the horns up over Davey's head."

Bobby looked proud yet sad, recalling Clifford's mischievousness and Davey's steadfastness. "It's a perfect picture," he says.

# CHAPTER 5

# The Labontes

> "Racing was just a hobby we did together. Instead of going fishing or going to the beach or going to the lake, we went racing."
>
> – Terry Labonte

When Terry Labonte wrapped up his second Winston Cup championship in 1996 at Atlanta Motor Speedway, Bobby won the race. The media members wanted Terry to talk about things he'd done with Bobby, but the Iceman couldn't think of anything. Car owner Rick Hendrick got a mischievous look on his face and said, "How about the truck story?" Terry ignored his boss at first, then gave him a "How could you?" look.

Finally, Terry told the truck story.

It seems Bob Labonte had this old truck that he wanted his boys to take to the junkyard. But, boys being boys — actually, they were grown men at this point — they decided they needed to do something special. They would shoot the truck. With a gun.

So they got Terry's pistol and pumped a few shots into the truck. It was great fun . . . until dad Bob Labonte called and said he'd changed his mind. He wanted the truck back. So the "boys" went into the sibling schtick, which went pretty much this way: "You shot the truck!" "Well, you did, too!" "Yeah, but it was *your* gun!"

Bob Labonte wasn't amused, but the members of the media were. The story reminded people of

the TV commercials featuring the two, and it humanized the Labontes, who are a lot less calm than they appear. Let's put it this way: Terry didn't get his nickname The Iceman from the truck story.

The central figure in this story is Bob Labonte, who was there when Terry began racing quarter-midgets in 1964 in their hometown of Corpus Christi, Texas, and in 1969 when Bobby took to quarter-midgets.

When Bobby won the 1991 Busch Grand National championship, he said his best time with his dad came that year. And it's almost certain that Terry and Bob Labonte enjoyed Terry's Winston Cup championship years in 1984 and '96.

Racing, you see, is a Labonte family project. Racing is their work, their recreation and their family business.

"Racing was just a hobby we did together," Terry says. "Instead of going fishing or going to the beach or going to the lake, we went racing."

Mention Terry Labonte, and three nicknames come to mind. First, he's the always-cool, always-calm Iceman, and he's "Texas Terry," a moniker that Bobby will throw his way occasionally. On April 21, 1996, at Martinsville (Virginia) Speedway, Terry earned a new nickname, "The Ironman," when he surpassed Richard Petty's NASCAR record for consecutive starts with No. 514. Labonte's amazing streak was at 637 starts through the 1999 season.

Texas Terry has been extremely successful at racing for thirty-five years. To make the big time, Terry hooked up with a Texan named Billy Hagan.

Driving Hagan's cars, Terry ran just four Winston Cup races in 1978, but he finished fourth in his first start, the 1978 Southern 500. This was remarkable, since Darlington (South Carolina) Raceway is proclaimed the track Too Tough to Tame, and Terry had nearly tamed it on his first try.

Terry was Corpus Christi Sportsman of the Year in 1979, the year he would lose out on Winston Cup rookie of the year honors. That wasn't too bad, though, since two of his fellow rookies were Dale Earnhardt and Harry Gant.

Earnhardt would win a race that year — something that rookies rarely do — and would win the championship the next year. But that's Earnhardt's story.

Terry would pull a surprise in 1980 and win the Southern 500. At Darlington. He'd win again in

Terry placed fourth in his first start, the 1978 Southern 500. Two years later Labonte surprised everyone by taking the checkered flag.

1983, in the fall race at North Carolina Motor Speedway in Rockingham. Then came 1984. Still driving Hagan's No. 44 Chevrolets, Labonte won twice, posted six second-place and six third-place finishes and won the Winston Cup championship.

The list of men behind Labonte in the standings would make the championship even sweeter.

Once Terry started racing, and winning trophies, younger brother Bobby wasn't far behind.

The No. 2 finisher that year? Harry Gant. And four former or future champions would finish behind Labonte and Gant: third-place Bill Elliott (the 1988 champion), Earnhardt (the seven-time champ), Darrell Waltrip (the three-time winner) and Bobby Allison (the '83 champ).

Terry and Hagan split up after the 1986 season, when Labonte was twelfth in points, and Terry joined car owner Junior Johnson, who had won three championships each with Cale Yarborough and Waltrip. Labonte and Johnson ran well together — third in points in 1987, fourth in '88 and tenth in '89 — and Terry won The Winston all-star race with Johnson in '88.

Terry switched to Richard Jackson's team in 1990. That didn't work, so he went back to Hagan

for three more years, 1991–93. Labonte didn't win this time for Hagan and his winless streak reached four years. The whispers circulated: Terry was done, finished.

But then he signed with Hendrick Motorsports in 1994, and the good times rolled again. Terry won three times in '94, and he added three more victories in 1995.

Then came 1996, a year that appeared to go in favor of Terry's young Hendrick Motorsports teammate, Jeff Gordon. While Gordon was cranking out a series-high ten victories, Labonte was typically cool and consistent. Gordon lost some hundred points to Labonte at Charlotte, North Carolina, that fall, and Terry calmly nipped Gordon by thirty-seven points for the title before heading to the Atlanta pressbox to tell the truck story.

And that brings us to Bobby Labonte, the winner that day in Atlanta. Bobby finished fourth in Grand National points and was the series' Most Popular Driver in 1990, his first full season in the series.

The next year, 1991, Bobby won the Busch Grand National championship and made two Winston Cup starts in his own car (not finishing either race).

In 1992, Bobby linked up with Bill Davis, and he did well enough to finish nineteenth in points and be the runner-up for rookie of the year. The top rookie? Some kid named Gordon.

Bobby didn't win in two seasons with Davis, but he was in position for a career-making move. When Dale Jarrett left Joe Gibbs Racing, Bobby claimed the reins of the No. 18 Pontiacs. He got his first three Winston Cup wins, and he was on his way.

In 1994, David Green won the Grand National championship while driving Bobby's cars. And, in 1995, the Labontes finished first and second in the

By age fifteen, Terry was winning regional and national quarter-midget meets and looking for a new challenge. Stock car racing appeared to be the next logical step.

Bob would get off work, come home, and spend the rest of the evening helping Terry build a winning race car.

same race twice, at Charlotte and Michigan, and the brothers won back-to-back races on two occasions, Pocono-Michigan and Michigan-Bristol.

Bobby posted single victories in 1996 and '97, then added two wins in 1998 and five in 1999. Bobby's seventh full Winston Cup season was an eye-opener, even though he suffered a broken shoulder blade in practice on March 19 at Darlington. He finished second in points to the man he replaced with Joe Gibbs Racing, Jarrett, and he became one of the favorites for the 2000 championship. Maybe *the* favorite.

Bobby, like Terry, is a consistent performer. Until 1999, when he was twelfth in Winston Cup points, Terry finished tenth or better sixteen times in his first twenty full-time seasons. Bobby finished tenth in Winston Cup points in 1995, eleventh in 1996, seventh in 1997 (one spot behind Terry), sixth in 1998 and second in '99.

And through it all, the Labontes have stayed close to each other and their families. Terry and Kim Labonte have two children, Justin (nineteen on February 5, 2000) and Kristen (seventeen on June 8, 2000), and they kept a close eye on the pro-

The Labonte family celebrated in style at the NASCAR awards banquet following Terry's first Winston Cup championship in 1984.

ceedings as Justin made his Grand National debut in 1999 at Nashville. And Bobby's wife, Donna, and young son, Tyler (six on April 18, 2000) keep close watch over the No. 18 car.

So it's clear no Labonte has lost the competitive fire needed to run with NASCAR's best. Perhaps the perfect example of this came in 1999. Terry posted his twenty-first victory on March 28 at Texas Motor Speedway, and, in the fall at Bristol, Tennessee, he was on the way to No. 22 right after passing his old hunting buddy Earnhardt. But Dale got a little too close — he said he wanted to rattle Terry's cage — and Terry crashed on the last lap. With Earnhardt celebrating in victory lane, Terry talked to the media. He didn't blow up. He calmly intimated that Earnhardt should be careful, *very* careful.

It was classic Labonte: hot and icy at the same time.

Bobby has worked with his father throughout his racing career, but never was the time more rewarding, he says, than during his run to the 1991 Busch series championship.

Bobby won a career-high five races in 1999, finishing a close second to Dale Jarrett in the Winston Cup series standings and establishing himself as a favorite for the 2000 title.

Nobody would want to be on the receiving end of one of the Iceman's cold stares — not even the Intimidator, Dale Earnhardt.

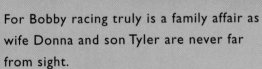

For Bobby racing truly is a family affair as wife Donna and son Tyler are never far from sight.

For Texas Terry, 1999 was a "down" year, characterized by only one win, seven top-ten finishes and $2,303,146 in earnings.

# EXTENDED FAMILIES

# CHAPTER 6

# The Andrettis

John Andretti smiles when he's asked about his famous racing family. When the Andrettis get together, John says, the last one to get hurt is the winner.

Competitive? Sure, the Andrettis are competitive. Put them in a car, and they want to win. Put them in go-karts or on bicycles, they want to win. Start a family reunion softball game, a badminton contest, or spelling bee . . . well, you get the idea.

The Andrettis are indeed winners. Mario Andretti, for instance, won fifty-two Indy-style races, including the 1969 Indianapolis 500. He won four Indy-car championships, the 1967 Daytona 500 and the 1978 Formula One championship. One son, Michael, was the 1991 CART champion, and the other son, Jeff, is a competitive open-wheel racer. And Mario's nephew, John, has won in many styles of racing.

Mario Gabriele Andretti was born on Febrary 28, 1940, in Montona, Italy. The Andretti family moved to Nazareth, Pennsylvania, in 1955, and he and wife Dee Ann were married in 1961. As the Andretti family grew, Mario raced and won and won.

It's fair to say that Mario Andretti is an American icon. Name the greatest American drivers ever, and Andretti's name joins a short list that includes Richard Petty, Dale Earnhardt and Andretti's Indy-car rival, A.J. Foyt. In fact, when *The Associated Press* named the top drivers of the

20th century as voted by a six-member panel of racing experts, Andretti tied Foyt for the top spot.

Yes, Andretti was and is a winner, but he's as famous for his failures as his successes. He won Indy in his fifth try (1969), and he tried and tried and tried for more than twenty more years to win again. He actually was declared the winner briefly one year following some scoring confusion, but the race later was awarded to Bobby Unser.

Andretti has been even more noticeable on television since his retirement. Perhaps most notable is the commercial where he talks about son Michael's first competitive pass on him. "Bye-bye, dada" is the memorable catchphrase that came from that commercial.

But don't think of Mario as a driver who has retired to a life of leisure and TV commercials. He has many business interests, plus a laundry list of hobbies.

Michael Mario Andretti is a great driver in his own right. He collected his thirty-eighth CART victory in 1999 at the Gateway International Raceway in Madison, Illinois, and is the winningest current series driver.

While Mario lists his Formula One championship as his favorite racing memory, Michael leans to his 1991 CART title. On a career-highlight day, Michael won at Leguna Seca, leading every lap, clinching the championship and finishing on the podium with Mario.

Mario Andretti's 1967 Daytona 500 victory was just the beginning of a spectacular career that included four Indy-car championships.

Jeff, who started out in the Pro-Formula Ford Series in 1983, is proud of being named the rookie of the year at Indy, but his favorite racing memory came at Pocono in 1986 when he won the Indy Lights race and Mario took the CART race the following day.

John, the son of Mario's twin brother, Aldo, is one of the few men to win Indy-car (Gold Coast Grand Prix and Australia in 1991) and Winston Cup (Daytona in 1997, and Martinsville in 1999) events. And he's the only man to win Winston Cup races, an Indy-car event and a twenty-four-hour race at Daytona (1989).

John was the first driver to compete in the Indy 500 and the Coca-Cola 600 in Charlotte, North Carolina, on the same day. And, while most drivers

say they enjoy watching drag racing, John Andretti made the semifinals in his first NHRA Winston Drag Racing Top Fuel event in 1993, beating Winston champion Joe Amato along the way.

John and Mario make a unique duo. The Andrettis are one of only three families to put multiple family members in Daytona's victory lane in Winston Cup, joining the Pettys (Lee and Richard) and the Allisons (Bobby, Donnie and Davey Allison).

John's proud of being an Andretti, of course, but, at heart, he's a joker. One year at a media gathering in Charlotte, John stood with his car owner, Richard Petty, and talked about the family aspect of his Winston Cup race team, Petty Enterprises. With a twinkle in his eye, he introduced himself as John AnPetty.

No matter. Whether it's AnPetty or Andretti, it's a talented and unique family. The Andrettis race hard, play hard. And they win — whatever the sport, and whatever the occasion.

In voting for the top drivers of the 20th century by a six-member panel of racing experts, Mario and A.J. Foyt tied for the top spot.

John is the only driver to win both Winston Cup and Indy-car events as well as a twenty-four-hour race at Daytona.

John continued to improve as a member of the Richard Petty Enterprises team in 1999, picking up his second Winston Cup victory at the Goody's Body Pain 500 at Martinsville Speedway.

# CHAPTER 7

# The Bakers

When fans start naming the top stock-car racing families, they often overlook the Bakers. And that's easy to do, considering Buck and Buddy's modest nature.

Elzie Wylie "Buck" Baker Sr. was working as a bus driver in Charlotte, North Carolina, when he attended his first stock-car race. He figured he, too, could drive, because he had done it most of his life.

But when Buck competed in his first race in 1939 at Greenville, South Carolina, fear took over. He realized, he recalled later, that the other drivers wanted to win as much as he did.

"But I didn't have to worry," he said. "A tire came off my car and I was lucky I got it off the track."

Buck Baker didn't stay scared long, and his tires generally stayed on the car the remainder of his illustrious career. In fact, he became one of NASCAR's well-respected pioneers.

Baker won the Winston Cup championship in 1956 and 1957, placed second in the final point standings twice (1955 and 1958) and finished in the top five on four other occasions. Baker ranks among the leaders in NASCAR starts (682) and victories (forty-six). He won the Southern 500 at Darlington (South Carolina) Raceway three times, in 1953, 1960 and 1964.

But remember that this was the Sixties. There was no Winston Million, no $8 million budgets for

The King, Richard Petty, strung together ten consecutive victories in 1967 before Buddy ended the streak with a win at Charlotte. Here the two prepare for the 1972 Winston 500 at Talladega.

race teams, no massive sponsorships through DuPont or GM Goodwrench, no title sponsorship by Winston. You weren't going to become rich racing NASCAR's top division, then called Grand National, so Baker found it cost-effective to drop to the Grand American division in 1967.

Naturally he excelled. In 1972, he started 109 races — yes, 109 — and won eight times. He's in several halls of fame and was a member of the inaugural class of the International Motorsports Hall of Fame in 1997.

Buck's son, Elzie Wylie "Buddy" Baker Jr., also became a major NASCAR star. Buddy, known as the "Gentle Giant" for his pleasant demeanor and six-foot-five frame, was quick with a smile and a quip, even if he wasn't so meek in a race car. He raced to win, and he was a monster at places such as Charlotte, Daytona and Talladega.

Buck (right) and Buddy, shown touting
their numbers for their 1962 Chrysler
300 cars, have combined for sixty-five
NASCAR victories. "Every day I'm overwhelmed that we both experienced our
dreams," Buddy says.

In fact Baker won the 1980 Daytona 500 from
the pole, setting a record pace of 177.602 miles per
hour. He was the first driver to exceed two hundred mph on an enclosed course (Talladega Superspeedway), and he was the driver who ended
Richard Petty's ten-race winning streak in 1967
when he won at Charlotte Motor Speedway.

Buddy, one of NASCAR's leading tire testers
for many years, started 688 Winston Cup races,
won nineteen, finished in the top five 198 times and
the top ten 299 times. He won forty poles and
more than $3.6 million.

Baker joined his dad as a member of the International Motorsports Hall of Fame in 1997, and
he's a member of several other halls of fame. Not

Buddy always exhibited poise under the toughest conditions. In the 1973 World 600, the Gentle Giant righted himself after blowing the right rear tire, pitted for a change, and went on to win the race.

surprisingly, Buddy says it wasn't easy following Buck Baker. As it was with Kyle Petty following Richard Petty or Larry Pearson following David Pearson, the expectations were suffocating.

"At the onset of my career, it came to be a handicap," he says. "Hey, I was being compared to one of the best drivers in the world, and second wasn't good enough — third certainly wasn't good enough. It took a while.

"I didn't stay with the family team. I did it the hard way, and I'm glad I did. It taught me the ins and outs of racing, and I wouldn't give that up for anything."

Buddy says sharing victory lane with Buck was a thrill. Sharing halls of fame is even better.

A few years ago, Buddy was flabbergasted when told by a writer that he was a candidate for the International Motorsports Hall of Fame. It got even worse when the well-spoken Buddy, now a long-time television broadcaster, was formally announced as a 1997 inductee. In the Darlington Raceway pressbox, Buddy rambled, barely able to explain his emotions. But they were deep.

"Every day I'm overwhelmed that we both experienced our dreams," he said in late 1999. "Not many can say that. I'm proud of my father. He's one of the top three drivers to drive in the sport.

"I'm amazed he and I shared so many things."

# CHAPTER 8

# The Bodines

If you've seen the movie *Days of Thunder*, you remember the scene where the two feuding drivers, Cole Trickle and Rowdy Burns, race rental cars through city streets on their way to meet the president of their sanctioning body.

It didn't happen exactly that way in real life. In the mid-1980s, Dale Earnhardt and Geoff Bodine were having a classic North-South spat. Bodine was the new Yankee from Chemung, New York, and Earnhardt was the rebellious Intimidator from Kannapolis, North Carolina. Their civil war raged on the track, and NASCAR chief Bill France Jr. called the two on the carpet.

They didn't use two rental cars. Instead, Geoff was driving the rental car, with Earnhardt riding shotgun. France was riding in a car in front, and Earnhardt was urging his rival to give Bill Jr.'s car a nudge.

This real-to-reel story utilized a little poetic license, and Geoff Bodine was immortalized in a roundabout way.

Bodine, who changed his name of preference to Geoffrey in 1999, began racing micro-midgets at his father's Chemung Speedrome when he was five years old. In the varied career that followed Bodine won a record fifty-five Modified races in one season, earned 1982 Winston Cup rookie of the year honors and won the 1986 Daytona 500 (when Earnhardt ran out of gas). He also won the 1987 International Race of Champions (IROC)

series and took the checkered flag in the Winston all-star race in 1994. Bodine, born April 18, 1949, has won eighteen career Winston Cup races and was named one of NASCAR's "50 Greatest Drivers" in 1998.

Geoff, or rather, Geoffrey, is one of the more innovative drivers, being the first one to use power steering and full-face helmets exclusively.

Brother Brett, who turned forty-one on January 11, 2000, followed Geoffrey onto the Chemung Speedrome at a young age. After Brett won a Modified championship in 1984, he and wife

The Bodines always have remained close, despite some roughhousing in the inaugural Brickyard 400 that led to Brett spinning out Geoffrey en route to a second-place finish.

Diane took a chance and moved south. Living in a mobile home outside Lowe's Motor Speedway near Charlotte, North Carolina, Brett found work as a mechanic.

Brett was working in the shop for car owner Rick Hendrick when Geoff (pre-Geoffrey) won the 1986 Daytona 500, and Brett drove one Winston Cup race for Hendrick that year. Along the way, Brett hooked up with the Thomas Brothers Grand National team, then tried Winston Cup with Hoss Ellington on a part-time basis in 1987. By 1988, Brett was a full-time Winston Cup dri-

New York's Finest: Geoffrey Bodine has won eighteen career Winston Cup races and was named one of NASCAR's "50 Greatest Drivers" in 1998.

Brett worked in car owner Rick Hendrick's shop while brother Geoff's career flourished. But Brett's time would come, in 1988, when he began racing Winston Cup on a full-time basis.

ver with Bud Moore (Geoffrey's car owner in 1992–93), and Brett, like Geoffrey, was on his way.

The highlight of Brett's career came in 1990 when he won the spring race at now-defunct North Wilkesboro (North Carolina) Speedway. Some people complained that Brett won on a scoring error. "All I know," Geoffrey said, "is that I kissed my brother in victory lane."

To preserve their futures and the futures of their families, Geoffrey and Brett tried Winston Cup ownership. In mid-1993, Geoffrey bought the No. 7 team that had been owned by the late Alan Kulwicki (the 1992 Winston Cup champion), and,

Geoffrey struggled on the Winston Cup circuit in 1999, cracking the top ten just twice.

Todd Bodine's success has been limited to the Busch Grand National circuit, where he has posted ten career victories.

in 1995, Brett bought the No. 11 outfit owned for years by NASCAR legend Junior Johnson (one of Geoffrey's car owners).

Alas, Brett entered the 2000 season with a car ownership deal. Geoffrey sold the No. 7 team to Jim Mattei and switched rides to Joe Bessey's No. 60 team. But a deal in which Brett would sell the No. 11 team to Richard Hilton and stay on as driver and team manager, fell through.

In recent years, the brothers have earned their due. Geoffrey was named a "Legend of The Glen" at Watkins Glen (New York) International Raceway in 1999, and Brett was inducted into the Modified Hall of Fame at Stafford, Connecticut, in 1998.

Todd, born February 27, 1964, followed his brothers into the family business and has had an up-and-down career. Erratic in the sense that he's

raced Busch Grand National, moved up to Winston Cup, then dropped back to Grand National. Todd has contended for the Busch championship a couple of times in recent years, and he entered the 2000 season with ten career victories.

Geoffrey's son Barry also looks to carry on the Bodine name in racing. Barry has driven on

the NASCAR Craftsman Truck series and filled in for his dad on the Busch Grand National series.

Of course, not every race involving the Bodines has produced a display of brotherly love. Take the inaugural Brickyard 400 in 1994, for instance, when Geoffrey and Brett took their little family feud to the track and made it public. While rac-ing for the lead, the brothers bumped a few times, and Brett was admonished later for spinning out his brother. Brett went on to finish second to Jeff Gordon — probably the second biggest finish of his career — and, eventually, the brothers made up.

After all, what's a little rough driving among brothers?

# CHAPTER 9

# The Burtons

The Burton brothers, Ward and Jeff, wear the entire sport of racing on their shoulders like an Eveready battery: They race hard, and they race to win. And sometimes they get a bit upset in the process.

Years ago, the two were involved in a wreck while racing on a short track not far from their home in South Boston, Virginia. Both brothers climbed out of their cars and a shoving match ensued.

Ward and Jeff cringe to this day when they're reminded of the race, and suffice it to say, they haven't shaken each other on the track since, unless you count some hard racing. These are two of the best drivers in Winston Cup, and they don't back down. Occasionally they'll rub fenders or one will finish directly ahead of the other.

In fact, Jeff and Ward finished 1–2, respectively, on three occasions in 1999. Ward, who turned thirty-eight on October 25, 1999, was miffed. He loves his little brother, of course, but, it's embarrassing to finish behind a sibling who is six years younger (Jeff turned thirty-two on June 29).

In 1999, Jeff and Ward were leading a race under caution, and Ward got playful. He pushed his Pontiac into Jeff's Ford, slightly lifting the rear wheels off the road. Ward laughed, while Jeff fumed. You don't play around with victory, he said, or something colorful to that effect.

Jeff picked up career Winston Cup victory No. 1 at the Interstate Batteries 500 in 1997 — the inaugural NASCAR event at Texas Motor Speedway — prompting a celebratory bear hug from Ward.

While Jeff has been piling up Winston Cup victories — he entered the 2000 season with eleven overall, six in 1999 alone — Ward had posted only one Cup win in the same period. That came in the fall of 1995 at North Carolina Speedway in Rockingham, and there have been dozens of top-five and top-ten finishes since for both brothers.

But Jeff has claimed all the victories, and it's hard to take for Ward, who has been a winner ever since he raced go-karts at age eight. Three years after that, five-year-old Jeff watched Ward race and wanted to race himself.

They had other interests, of course. Ward played baseball and basketball at Hargrave Mili-

tary Academy, where he was a 1st lieutenant. He earned first place on the rifle team at Hargrave, and he remains a passionate outdoorsman, involved in everything from hunting and shooting skeet to boating.

Jeff, meanwhile, was an outstanding athlete at Halifax County (Virginia) Senior High School, playing basketball and captaining the soccer team. But while Ward is an outdoorsy guy, Jeff prefers to spend his free time rooting for the Duke Blue Devils and Carolina Panthers.

Still, neither Burton could do without racing. Both brothers developed their skills, and a passion for the sport, racing Street Stocks and Late Model Stocks on Virginia short tracks, mainly South Boston Speedway.

Ward was a winning Busch Grand National driver for four years, then made his Winston Cup debut in 1994 for fellow Virginian Alan Dillard. He has been driving for Bill Davis Racing since late 1995.

Jeff won twenty-one Winston Racing Series events before moving up to Busch. He made his Winston Cup debut (qualifying sixth at Loudon, New Hampshire) in 1993, and he was Winston Cup rookie of the year the next season while driving for the Stavola Brothers. (One of the guys who finished behind Jeff was Ward.) Jeff ran well for the Stavolas, but his career took off after he switched to Jack Roush Racing in 1996.

Jeff picked up his first three wins in 1997 and finished fourth in points. He dropped back to two wins and fifth in points the next year, but he came back with the monster year in '99. He led the points race early in the season and wound up fifth with five victories, including wins in both Charlotte races, and more than $5 million in winnings.

The Burtons, like most racers, spend much of their time off the track with fans, sponsors, the media and charities. As for charities, Ward favors the Ward Burton Wildlife Foundation and the Patrick Henry School for Boys and Girls, while Jeff contributes to the South Boston Jaycees and Give the Kids the World Foundation.

So, at heart, the Burtons really are wonderful guys — just as long as they're not trading paint on a racetrack.

Jeff joined the Winston Cup series in 1993 and was named the Winston Cup rookie of the year in 1994 as a member of the Stavola Brothers team. Ward made the jump to Winston Cup in 1994 as well and has been chasing his little brother ever since.

Ward came up a car short of his second career victory three times in 1999 . . .

...All three times Jeff took the checkered flag. "It's hard to go out there and one of your goals is to beat your brother," Jeff told *NASCAR Online*.

Many NASCAR insiders believe it's only a matter of time before Ward wins his first race since 1995. Nobody would be happier than brother Jeff.

# CHAPTER 10

# The Flocks

**T**im Flock once recalled a race in the mid-1950s on the beach/road course at Daytona Beach. Flock had the pole, but he wasn't exactly sure what was going to happen.

The flag flew, Flock gunned the engine . . . and he plunged headlong into a flock of birds. Dozens, maybe hundreds. Who knows? It might have been thousands of white birds. He looked back, he said, and saw nothing but cars, white feathers and blood.

Flock would win that Chrysler 300 after another driver was disqualified, and the drivers came up with an ingenious plan the following year. They put two strips of plastic on their windshields.

When they hit the birds, they reached out and pulled off one strip. After seawater destroyed the second layer of plastic, they pulled it off. Windshield wipers had to handle the rest of the surf.

Tim, a member of the famed Flock racing family, had lots of winning moments during his hall-of-fame career. He was a two-time champion, first in 1952 while driving the legendary Hudson Hornet and again in 1955, while campaigning a Chrysler 300 for Carl Kiekhaefer. In '55, he won eighteen races and eighteen poles, records then thought unbreakable. Overall, Flock won forty races, tying him with Bill Elliott for fourteenth on NASCAR's all-time list.

Julius Timothy Flock took to cars and racing naturally. His father was a noted bicycle racer and

The Fabulous Flock Brothers (from left): Bob, Tim, Fonty and Carl.

owned the first car in Ft. Payne, Alabama. His older brother, Carl, raced boats before switching to real estate, and two other brothers, Bob and Fonty, also were standout drivers as members of the "Fabulous Flock Brothers."

But there were more Flocks: Younger sister Reo was an aerial daredevil and expert skeet shooter, while Ethel also pursued stock-car driving.

Tim saw his first race in 1937, and he loved it. His brothers told him he'd have to wait, so he worked at various jobs (taxi driver, fireman, bell-

hop and parking-lot attendant) in his hometown of Atlanta.

In 1948, Tim raced a car owned by Ethel and her husband. He won for the first time in a thirty-five-lap feature at North Wilkesboro, North Carolina, and he decided he would make racing his livelihood. He did well at it, moving up to Late Model Stocks owned by Ted Chester.

In 1952, Flock battled Herb Thomas (the champion in 1951 and '53), but, once the season-finale rolled around at West Palm Beach, Florida, Tim

When Tim (left) won a record eighteen races in 1955, his feat was thought to be unbreakable. Flock won forty races in all, ranking him fourteenth on NASCAR's all-time list.

Bob, the eldest of the Flock brothers, won four Winston Cup races in thirty-six career starts.

only needed to start to win the title. He started, but maybe he shouldn't have. On lap sixty-four, Flock's Hudson hit the retaining wall and flipped over, skidding down the frontstretch on its roof.

"I bet I'm the only guy who ever won a championship while on his head," said Tim, who won eight of thirty-four races that year.

In 1955, Flock had a remarkable year. He led every lap on eleven occasions, he won a record nineteen poles, and his eighteen victories were the standard until Richard Petty won twenty-seven in 1967. Naturally, Tim won his second championship.

Tim was the most successful of the Flocks, but Fonty (Truman Fontell) won nineteen Winston Cup races and finished second twenty times in 154 starts. Bob, the eldest of the trio who died in 1964, won four Winston Cup races in thirty-six career starts. Fonty, who died in 1972, won the first Modified race at Bowman Gray Stadium in Winston-Salem, North Carolina, and Tim was the first champion, in 1949.

Tim apparently was the joker of the family. In 1953, the monkey Jocko Flocko rode with Flock as his co-pilot for eight races, but Jocko went ape one time — he was a monkey, after all — so Tim had to park the car to let him out. Jocko was retired, but Tim had stories to tell for more than four decades.

Tim retired early and spent the rest of his life as an ambassador for the sport. He is a member of several halls of fame, but perhaps the most memorable came late in life. In 1998, NASCAR kicked off its 50th Anniversary celebration, and the Winston Cup visited the site of the first NASCAR-sanctioned Winston Cup race, held in Charlotte, North Carolina.

Tim, who had moved to the Charlotte area, was enjoying himself while regaling media members with stories. But, sadly, the last of Flock brothers learned about a month later that he had terminal cancer of the liver and throat.

Fonty, winner of the first Modified race in Winston-Salem, North Carolina, took the checkered flag nineteen times during his Winston Cup career.

Before his death on March 31, 1998, the North Carolina Auto Racing Hall of Fame inducted Flock into its ranks. The hall normally inducts only one person per year, and Bobby Allison already was slated for induction that year.

But for one of the "Fabulous Flock Brothers," the members were willing to make an exception.

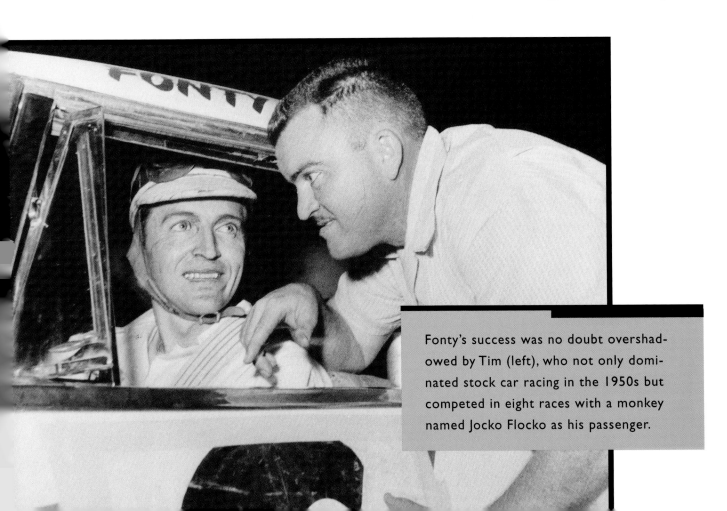

Fonty's success was no doubt overshadowed by Tim (left), who not only dominated stock car racing in the 1950s but competed in eight races with a monkey named Jocko Flocko as his passenger.

# CHAPTER 11

# The Frances

**B**ig-time stock car racing began, believe it or not, in Washington, D.C. before taking a long detour to Florida.

You see, William Henry Getty France was born in 1909 and grew up in the D.C. area, and it would be up to France to carry racing into the big time.

As a youngster, Bill loved racing. He'd play hooky from school so he could watch the races at the high-banked board track in Laurel, Maryland. He'd even take the family car out on the boards for a few laps, and, with a twinkle in his eye, he'd drive the Model-T to the tire dealer afterward to complain about worn tires.

France became a service station owner, but he decided it would be easier to get customers' cars started in warm weather. So he loaded up wife Anne, young son Bill Jr., a set of tools and twenty-five dollars into a Hupmobile and headed for Florida. He liked Daytona Beach and decided to settle there.

In 1936, the city of Daytona Beach lost money promoting a stock-car race. The Elks Club did the same the next year. Since France was a racer and racers gathered at his service station, he was asked to promote the next event.

Back then, Big Bill — all six-foot-five of him — was a racer.

He'd won a 1940 national stock-car championship, and he loved everything about the sport. But he had bigger dreams than just going around

In 1947 the National Association for Stock Car Auto Racing is formed during a three-day meeting chaired by Bill France at the Streamline Hotel in Daytona Beach. Rules, a points system, a driver's fund and a full schedule of races are put in place, bringing order to the chaos that is stock car racing.

in circles, so he gave up racing for the challenge of promotion.

First, France tried to get some help from a promoter in Orange City, Florida, but when France's fifteen-cent collect call was refused, he decided to do it himself.

On December 14, 1947, France called an organizational meeting at the Streamline Hotel in Daytona Beach. They were starting from nothing, but soon the National Association for Stock Car Auto Racing would be racing hard and everywhere.

First, though, the group organized events for the Daytona beach/road course. It wasn't easy, because the races had to be timed between the tides. You needed plenty of room for drivers to race and onlookers to watch.

Bill and Anne France did it all. Bill promoted the product vigorously, and he kept a close watch on the rules and the drivers. They did it his way or no way at all. Anne, meanwhile, handled the business side and the fine details.

Whether at Daytona Beach or on the road, Big Bill would pace the grounds and come up with one idea after another. Anne would sell tickets from a car.

But Bill France realized that racing on the road/beach course and other small venues wouldn't realize his dream. He wanted to build an enclosed, banked track in Daytona Beach, but that presented problems. How do you lay asphalt on a dirt bank? France solved the problem, and the 2.5-mile Daytona International Speedway opened in 1959.

Bill France Sr. handed over NASCAR's reins to Bill Jr. in 1972. Under Bill Jr.'s control, the sanctioning body continued to flourish.

A decade later, Big Bill decided to build an even bigger track at Talladega, Alabama. The 2.66-mile Talladega Superspeedway opened, and the drivers boycotted over concerns about the near-two hundred mph speeds and subsequent tire problems. But, with France leading the way, the race went on.

Since then, Talladega has become famous as the world's fastest speedway, and the International Motorsports Hall of Fame stands proudly on the grounds.

With pride and care, the Frances built an organization that now includes a vigorous marketing arm and the International Speedway Corp., which oversees everything from racetracks such as the Daytona, Darlington and Talladega tracks to Motor Racing Network (MRN) and DAYTONA USA. Daytona is the World Center of Racing, and the Daytona 500 is the sport's top event.

Several generations of Frances run the business. Bill France Jr. serves as chairman of the board and chief executive officer of ISC, while Jim France is president and Lesa Kennedy is executive vice president.

Bill France Jr. entertains President Reagan during the 1984 Daytona Beach Firecracker. Reagan became the first president to attend a stock car race.

With the help of Mike Helton, France Jr. oversees an empire that races in many divisions and at more than a hundred venues. Winston Cup is the flagship series, of course, but the other touring divisions range from Busch Grand National to Featherlite Modified. The Saturday night bullrings on the Weekly Racing Series stretch from Florida to New England to Alaska to California.

But mention NASCAR and its roots and it comes back to Big Bill France, who died in 1992.

In 1990, France was a member of the inaugural class of the International Motorsports Hall of Fame. It was a fitting gesture. You can't have a hall of fame without the guy who started it all.

When Big Bill's fifteen-cent collect call to a Florida promoter was refused, he decided to take matters into his own hands.

Jim France (left), shown with Richmond International Raceway founder Paul Sawyer, serves as the president of the International Speedway Corporation.

France Jr. announced that he was seeking treatment for cancer in December 1999, but wasn't relinquishing control of NASCAR or the ISC just yet.

# CHAPTER 12

# The Unsers

**M**ention most racing families, and it's pretty easy to name the top driver in the family: Richard Petty, Bobby Allison, David Pearson, Mario Andretti.

Name the Unsers, however, and you're in for a few headaches. There are lots of Unsers, and they're all good. Very good.

There's Alfred Unser Sr., the two-time Indy-car champion and four-time Indianapolis 500 winner. Al won thirty-nine races, twenty-seven poles and more than $6 million before retiring from the Indy-car circuit in 1992.

There's Bobby Unser, Al's older brother, who won the Indy 500 three times and finished second in Indy-car points twice. Bobby, born February 20, 1934, collected thirty-five career Indy-car wins and was the first driver to break 190 mph at Indianapolis. Most impressively, he won the Pikes Peak Hill Climb an amazing thirteen times.

Bobby, born in 1934, and Al Sr., born in 1939, are both members of the International Motorsports Hall of Fame.

Then there's Al Unser Jr., the Indy-car champion in 1990 and 1994, the Indy 500 champion in 1992 and 1994, the Driver of the Year in 1990, and a winner of the 24 At Daytona race in 1985 and 1986. He's also the winningest International Race of Champions driver and a former champion of the all-star series, and he has posted more than thirty Indy-car wins.

For the year 2000, Al Jr. will switch from the CART series to the Indy Racing Series and will make his first appearance at Indy in years.

Al Jr., known affectionately as Little Al, loves and respects his elders, especially Al Sr. "He's taught me everything I know," Al Jr. said on his Website, alunserjr.com, "but he hasn't taught me everything he knows."

Still, Little Al learned at age twenty that he could race with the big boys when he made his Indy-car debut at Riverside.

"Next to my Dad and Uncle Bobby, the drivers I always admired most were A.J. Foyt and Gordon Johncock," Little Al said on his site. "But in that first race I lapped A.J., I lapped Gordon, and I passed my dad. It was like I lost something. It was the day I knew I was one of them. I couldn't look at them that way ever again."

But these aren't the only successful Unser racers. Louis Unser (Uncle Louie) won the Pikes Peak Hill Climb nine times in thirty-six starts.

Joe Unser also showed promise but was killed early in his racing career test driving a FWD Coleman Special. Jerry Unser contributed to racing by fathering another important generation of racing Unsers (twins Jerry Jr. and Louis J., Bobby and Al).

Louis Unser, one of the twins born on November 15, 1932, is a top engine builder.

Al Unser Sr. won two Indy-car championships, four Indianapolis 500s and more than $6 million before retiring in 1992. "He's taught me everything I know," Al Unser Jr. says, "but he hasn't taught me everything he knows."

Jerry Jr., the other twin, was twenty-seven when he crashed in Turn 4 at Indy in 1959. When Bobby, then twenty-five, visited Jerry in the hospital the day before he died, Jerry was more interested in finding a ride for Bobby than talking about his recovery. Alas, Jerry never saw Bobby race again; he died on May 17, 1959.

Bobby, perhaps the most flamboyant of the Unsers, made his Indy 500 debut at age twenty-nine, but he finished a total of three laps in his first two Indy 500s. The next year, he finished sixty-nine laps before going out early with mechanical problems.

But Bobby went on to win Indy in 1968, 1975 and 1981, thus winning the race in three different decades. Bobby's 1981 Indy 500 victory is particularly memorable because of the political and legal battle that took place. At first, Bobby was the win-ner. But overnight USAC penalized him a lap, and Mario Andretti was handed his second Indy win. In October of that year, a special appeals panel voted 2–1 to give the victory back to Bobby.

Al Sr., who first drove Modified roadsters in 1957 in Albuquerque at age eighteen, finished second in his first Pikes Peak Hill Climb, in 1960. The winner? Bobby Unser.

Since retiring, Bobby has kept busy. He has worked on television broadcasts, and his interests include snowmobiling and flying, among his various projects.

Then there's the current generation of Unsers, Johnny and Robby, a pair of IRL drivers. Johnny, Jerry Jr.'s son, has been successful in several series, and Robby, Bobby's son, won his first Pikes Peak "Race to the Clouds" in 1990.

It's a bit confusing, trying to keep up with the Unsers. So many. So fast. So successful.

Bobby overcame early troubles at the Indy 500, winning the prestigious race in 1968, 1975 and 1981.

Little Al, a two-time Indy-car champ and two-time winner of the Indy 500, made the switch from CART to the IRL for the 2000 season, making possible his first appearance at the Indy 500 since 1995.

Third generation drivers Johnny (left) and Robby are the future of Unser racing. Johnny competed in fourteen IRL races in 1999, finishing in the top ten twice, while Robby placed in the top five three times.

At least one Unser has driven in the Indy 500 thirty-six of the past thirty-seven years.

# CHAPTER 13

# The Wallaces

It's a variation on the same old story: Papa goes racing, and the kids tag along.

Russ Wallace would run tracks such as the Tri-City Speedway in Granite City, Illinois, and Lakehill Speedway in Valley Park, Missouri, and wild-haired son Rusty would follow along. Soon afterward brothers Mike and Kenny followed, and the Wallace racing family was complete.

Mike, now a winning Craftsman Truck series driver, compares racing to hunting and fishing. If Dad shows interest in a sport, so, too, will the children.

Rusty and Mike started helping Russ Wallace at the track when they were teens. Kenny, the youngest of the Wallace brothers, says he hated watching from the sidelines. He simply wasn't old enough to go into the pits.

Still, Russ gave him a job changing gears and cleaning brakes on the dirt-track cars. Kenny felt important, and Russ enjoyed a measure of peace around the household.

Kenny, like Rusty and Mike, loved watching Russ race. He'd race night after night, and the boys would be there. When Russ Wallace fashioned a winning streak, the boys would revel in it, wishing all the while that they could race.

As teenagers, the brothers started a company called "Poor Boy Chassis" and built dirt-track cars for sale. But the three weren't content building cars.

Rusty's Winston Cup series debut came in 1984. He finished second in his first start, setting the stage for a remarkable NASCAR run.

Rusty made his debut at Lakehill Speedway in 1973, earning that year's Central Auto Racing Association rookie of the year award. He won more than two hundred feature races from 1974 to 1978 before joining the United States Auto Club's stock-car circuit in 1979. He won five races, was second in points and earned the USAC's rookie of the year award in '79.

Soon after, he joined the American Speed Association (ASA) circuit, and in 1983, he won the series championship.

Rusty broke into the Winston Cup series full-time in 1984 with owner Cliff Stewart, finishing second in his first start, at Atlanta. He switched to Raymond Beadle in 1986, winning two races in each of the next two seasons.

In 1988, Rusty won six races and two poles, finished second to Bill Elliott and got ready for his big push in 1989.

That year, Rusty became a household name. Still driving for Beadle, Wallace edged legend-in-the-making Dale Earnhardt by twelve points to win the Winston Cup championship. He won six races and more than $2.2 million, and, along the way, Wallace gained notoriety by spinning out Darrell Waltrip to win The Winston all-star race at Charlotte (North Carolina) Motor Speedway.

Rusty made a bold career move in 1991, hooking up with car owner/racetrack owner Roger Penske and Penske Racing South. He posted ten- and eight-win seasons in 1993-94, respectively, and finished his 1999 campaign with forty-nine career victories.

Mike, meanwhile, began racing at the age of sixteen, and he won more than three hundred races on short tracks throughout the Midwest. He posted twenty-one wins and five second-place finishes in 1990 and was the Mid-America Region champion of the NASCAR Winston Racing Series.

Rusty, no doubt, has enjoyed the most success in the Wallace family. The future Hall of Famer has won forty-nine Winston Cup races and a Cup series championship in 1989. "We're proud of Rusty, and he's proud of the success we've shared at other levels," Mike says.

He moved on to Busch Grand National and finished sixth in his first start at Martinsville [Virginia] Speedway. He had three career Busch wins, fifteen top-five and thirty-eight top-ten finishes in his first 119 starts.

Mike has scored his most success, though, in the ARCA Bondo/Mar-Hyde Series, posting six victories, twelve top-fives and thirteen top-tens.

Mike made his Winston Cup debut driving for Jimmy Means in 1991 and Junie Donlavey in 1994. By 1996, Wallace was looking for a ride again, and fellow Missourian Ken Schrader stepped up. Schrader, himself a long-time Winston Cup driver, gave Wallace a ride in the Craftsman Truck series.

So far, Mike has trucked right along. He won the 1999 season-opener at Homestead, then took the truck race at Pikes Peak, finishing the season sixth in series points.

Kenny didn't start racing until he was twenty-two. Like his brothers, Kenny raced ASA. He finished eleventh in points and earned top-rookie honors.

With Rusty's help, Kenny ran Busch Grand National and was rookie of the year in 1989. In 1991, Bobby Labonte beat him for the series title by only three points.

Eight Busch victories later, Kenny Wallace moved up to Winston Cup. He posted three top-ten finishes in 1993, his first full season with Felix Sabates. He moved to Filbert Martocci's team in late 1995, then joined Andy Petree Racing in 1999. Like Mike, Kenny entered 2000 with no Winston Cup victories.

No, the Wallaces haven't had equal success. Rusty's a probable future Hall-of-Famer; Mike and Kenny have struggled for their success.

Rusty's shadow probably has enveloped Kenny the most. Kenny, for example, was pleased with himself at Darlington Raceway in 1994. Ernie Irvan had gotten hurt two weeks earlier at Brooklyn, Michigan, and Kenny was given the opportunity to drive the No. 28 Ford Thunderbird that week. He qualified well and thought: "Good-bye, Shadow!"

"I managed to qualify in the top ten. I was proud of this, of course, and excited," Kenny recalls. "I had my Texaco-Havoline uniform on, and I felt big-time. I went into Rusty's trailer, looking for approval, and he looks at me and tells me to make him a bologna and cheese sandwich. That brought me down to earth fast."

Kenny, the youngest of the three Wallace brothers, wasn't old enough to help his father in the pits during the late 1960s. So Russ gave Kenny the task of changing gears and cleaning brakes around the house.

Mike won a pair of races and finished sixth in points in the 1999 Craftsman Truck series.

But did Kenny fill Rusty's order?

"Hell, yeah, I did it," little brother says fiercely.

Mike, on the other hand, says it hasn't been so bad being Rusty's little brother. "I don't think that Kenny or I will ever have the degree of success at the Winston Cup level that Rusty has," he says, "but there's no jealousy or animosity towards him about that. We're proud of Rusty, and he's proud of the success we've shared at other levels. We know that we don't have to prove anything to each other anymore."

Occasionally they'll be at the same track on the same weekend. Or they'll phone. They're brothers, and they still care a lot. And they race hard, just like dad.

Kenny enjoyed a breakthrough year in 1999, claiming three top-five finishes — but the driver of the No. 55 Square D Chevrolet is still searching for his first Winston Cup victory.

# CHAPTER 14

# The Waltrips

Darrell has won eighty-four career races, tying him for third on the all-time list with Bobby Allison.

**M**ichael Waltrip remembers growing up in Owensboro, Kentucky, in the 1970s and being so proud of big brother Darrell. While Michael was going through adolescence, Darrell was racing future hall-of-famers Richard Petty, David Pearson, Benny Parsons, Buddy Baker, Bobby Allison and Cale Yarborough . . . and he was winning. Big-time winning.

Darrell, who is sixteen years Michael's senior, started racing go-karts in 1959, and he moved to Late Model Sportsman in the early 1960s. In 1972, when Michael was nine, Darrell made his first Winston Cup start in the Winston 500 at Talladega, Alabama.

Soon, the victories started coming. Darrell won twice in 1975, at Nashville (his "home track") and Richmond, and he won at least one race every year after up to 1989. His 1981 and '82 seasons, with Junior Johnson, were milestone years: Waltrip won twelve races each year and won two Winston Cup titles. Darrell claimed another title with Junior in 1985, a year famous for Bill Elliott collecting eleven victories, eleven poles and the Winston Million.

Along the way, Darrell became the brash upstart and earned the nickname "Jaws." Once, Darrell responded to being booed by telling fans to meet him down at the Kmart parking lot for a discussion. That statement would haunt him years

later, when Kmart became his sponsor with Travis Carter's team.

But a lot happened in the interim. When Waltrip won the 1989 Daytona 500, the showman did a dance and spiked his helmet in victory lane. He nearly won the Winston Million that year, and two years later he started his own team. He started strong, winning twice in 1991 and three times in 1992.

In the 1992 Southern 500 at Darlington, Waltrip was waiting out a rain delay with the lead, so he did a little rain dance. The race ended with the cars covered up on pit road, and Waltrip collected career victory No. 84, moving him ahead of Yarborough and tying him with Allison for third place all-time.

But the victories stopped there, and Waltrip sold his race team a few years later. In 2000 the now-venerable DW will cap a sure-fire hall-of-fame career with Kmart as his sponsor.

Perhaps the prouder moments for Waltrip since 1992 have been fatherhood (Sarah Kaitlyn and Jessica Leigh) and a new reputation as the grand-ole-man of racing (he turned fifty-three on February 5, 2000). Like Jack Nicklaus, Waltrip has gone from the pushy upstart to one of the revered giants.

**1 2 3**

Racing enthusiasts probably will always remember Darrell's victory in the 1989 Daytona 500 — and resulting victory lane celebration.

Then there's the opportunity to race with Michael. The younger Waltrip started racing go-karts in the late 1970s, and he tried stock cars in 1981. He was the NASCAR Dash Series champion in 1983, and he made his Winston Cup debut in the 1985 World 600 at Charlotte.

Michael, like Darrell, is a great talker, which gets him regular gigs on television shows. Unlike his brother, though, Michael has never won a Winston Cup points race. In fact, he's started 428 races through the 1999 season without a victory.

He's had his moments, though. One year, Michael won a Busch Grand National race at Charlotte, and he stood on his head in victory lane. He also had one of the most horrific wrecks

in NASCAR history, when his car hit the end of a guardrail at Bristol Motor Speedway. The car was demolished and everyone feared the worst. When Michael stood up, the front end of the car was so compressed that he was in the back half of the car.

But Michael, who turned thirty-six on April 30, 1999, tries to laugh off the non-victories. He did win The Winston all-star race at Charlotte in 1996, but, as he points out, "It wasn't a *points* race. I haven't won a *points* race."

Michael's career highlight, though, may have come right *after* he won The Winston. In Charlotte's victory lane, the six-foot-one Darrell joined his little brother, looking both gleeful and tearful as he hugged the six-foot-five Michael.

Most of all, he looked proud.

Michael won the Winston Open in 1991 and 1992, but he still hasn't visited victory lane in a Winston Cup points race. No other active driver has started more races (428 through 1999) without his first victory.

Darrell and Michael have formed their own mutual admiration society. Neither could be prouder of the other's racing accomplishments.

Jessica Leigh was less than two years old when her father won the Daytona 500 in 1989. Three years later Jessica's sister Sarah Kaitlyn was born.

Michael has proven that success is possible without winning on the Winston Cup circuit. The Kentucky native has earned more than $9 million in fourteen full Cup seasons.

# PHOTO CREDITS